C0-DAU-004

A Family in Holland

This book takes you on a trip to the legendary tulip fields of Holland. There you will meet the Roozen family who have been growing tulips for over 200 years. Leo Roozen will show you around the business and explain how he produces new varieties of flowers. You will also discover what the rest of the family do, what their home is like, what they like to eat, and what their interests are.

FAMILIES AROUND THE WORLD

A FAMILY IN
HOLLAND

Peter Otto Jacobsen and
Preben Sejer Kristensen

The Bookwright Press
New York · 1984

Families Around the World

A Family in France
A Family in Holland
A Family in India
A Family in Mexico

First published in the United States in 1984 by
The Bookwright Press, 387 Park Avenue South
New York, NY 10016

First published in 1984 by
Wayland (Publishers) Limited
49 Lansdowne Place, Hove
East Sussex BN3 1HF, England

ISBN 0–531–03789–4
Library of Congress Catalog Card Number: 84–70779

Printed in Italy by G. Canale and C.S.p.A., Turin

Contents

By train to Holland

We are at the main railroad station in Brussels, the capital city of Belgium, boarding the train for Amsterdam in Holland. From there we shall travel to Haarlem, just outside Amsterdam, and then to the famous tulip fields, to meet a family who have been in the business of growing tulips for more than 200 years.

The trip will not take too many hours, and we can sit back in the clean, comfortable train and watch the flat, sunlit countryside flashing past as we speed on our way north into Holland.

The kingdom of Holland (or the Netherlands) is a small country bordered by West Germany in the east, Belgium in the south, and the cold North Sea in the west and north. Two-fifths of the land has been reclaimed from the sea. These areas are known as polder-lands. A coastal belt of sand dunes, planted with strong grass, helps protect the country from flooding, and dikes are extra protection at more vulnerable places.

Looking out of the train window we catch sight of herons and other wading birds that live along the straight, man-made canals crisscrossing the countryside. The canals help drain the land, and some lie above sea level. Along many of the bigger canals we see wooden barges moored close together, and we spot a ship

Many people live and work on Holland's waterways.

Sheep and cows grazing on fertile land.

on a canal that looks as if it is sailing through the fields! Many of Holland's goods are carried from place to place along its network of waterways.

Our train is slowing down as it travels through the outskirts of Amsterdam, and finally pulls in to the Central Station.

From north to south Holland is approximately 300 kilometers (186 miles). From west to east it is about 260 kilometers (162 miles).

Amsterdam and Haarlem

Amsterdam, the Venice of northern Europe.

The city of Amsterdam is one of the most picturesque in Europe. It began in the Middle Ages as a settlement at the mouth of the Amstel River, and became a flourishing merchant city. Like Venice, it is a city built on water. Along the tree-lined canals are tall, ornate, merchants' houses dating back to the seventeenth century. Today they are offices and banks. Bridges of every design span the water at frequent intervals, and houseboats bob up and down on the canals. Amsterdam is full of history but it is also a thriving modern industrial center.

We find our platform for the train to Haarlem. The journey will only take about 20 minutes from the bustle of Amsterdam to the tranquility of the countryside. We buy some fruit and a cup of coffee from the refreshment trolley on the platform, before boarding our train.

The sun is going down as we arrive in Haarlem. All is very peaceful as the sounds of the old church clock striking ring out in the big market square. Outside the cosy restaurants there are tables and chairs set out under brightly colored awnings, and we sit and enjoy a cup of delicious coffee while slowly shaking off the long journey.

After a night in a small hotel we are up early to continue on our way. We walk through the narrow streets and across bridges over the canals, past picturesque old houses and tiny cobbled lanes. Finally we come to the long main street with its hundreds of stores that spill out on to the pavements. Although it is early, the place is bustling with activity and full of people. There are countless shoe stores, next door to food stores selling all kinds of cooked meats, cheeses, and the

Market day in Haarlem.

An attractive store-window display of Dutch delicacies.

10

The tulips of Holland are world-famous.

In the month of April, the small villages nestle in a gigantic flowerbed of tulips of every variety and color – even black tulips. Vogelenzang, where we are headed, is one of these villages which literally blooms once a year.

Vogelenzang is in the heart of the tulip fields.

unique Dutch delicacy of raw, salted herrings. Just off the main street we find a fascinating antique shop, full of beautiful furniture, maritime instruments, and all kinds of things that beg to be bought.

Outside the town lie the legendary tulip fields. We find our way to the bus depot and have no problem in finding a bus that will take us the short ride to where the famous bulbs have been cultivated for over 200 years.

11

We meet the Roozen family

The bus halts in a country road, and we climb down to be greeted by the Roozen family. They have been waiting for us in front of their two-story house, that faces onto the road leading into Vogelenzang.

Leo Roozen and his wife, Sylvia, have two children; Evelien who is four, and Bas, who is only two. The fifth member of the family is a large golden labrador, called Janni. We shake hands enthusiastically with all of them in the typical Dutch manner. As a nation, the Dutch are great handshakers, and if you met a Dutchman for the first time he would probably accompany his handshake with a small, formal bow.

"First, come and see how we grow tulips," says Leo.

"And come into the house afterwards for some coffee," adds Sylvia.

We promise not to be too long. Sylvia takes the children indoors, and we follow Leo on our tour of inspection.

Leo speaks excellent English like most Dutch people. It is vital for a small country that trades with other nations to be fluent in foreign languages, and most children learn English, French and German in school.

Behind the house are the flower exhibition halls; to one side is a very attractive garden with a carp pool, and on the other

The Roozen family outside their house.

side is a large building where the tulips are stored and dried. From the garden you can gaze on the colorful tulip fields stretching over six hectares (15 acres).

Leo carries on the family business. His special interest is in creating new varieties of tulips.

Leo is 32 years old, and his family have been growing tulips since 1780. In the last forty or fifty years they have created about a hundred different varieties. It was Leo's parents who first began cross-breeding different varieties in the 1940s, and Leo continues this work today.

The tulip industry

The seeds which result from cross-pollination are dried and stored in the seed houses.

Leo takes us first into one of the seed houses. He is eager to show us how he creates new varieties of tulips.

"Trying to develop new varieties is one of my hobbies, but it takes years for a new bulb to flower and to see the result. In actual fact I do exactly the same as the bees. I take the pollen from one flower and transfer it to the bloom of another. The seeds which it produces are then dried and placed on trays in here, where they stay for two years. If we are lucky we may then get a small bulb," explains Leo.

"To grow a variant which will be successful, depends not only on its shape and color, but also on how robust the plant is against disease. It is a question of expertise, luck and, last but not least, patience," he smiles.

Next, Leo shows us around the big exhibiting halls where the customers can see the flowers, the garden and the building where the bulbs are stored. He tells us about his work with the tulips.

"We plant the bulbs in November. This is done by machinery, and takes three men ten days. Then the winter comes, when we fertilize and weed. That's the part of the year when we have the least work, so that's the time we take

Customers can walk around the garden and display halls to see the different varieties of tulips.

our annual vacation.

"In the early part of March we spray the bulbs against infection, and when they bloom in April we take out any diseased ones. At the end of April and the beginning of May we cut the flowers. This gives us bigger and more bulbs.

"We dig the tulip bulbs up at the end of June and dry them, peel them, and sort the large ones from the small ones. Then they are put in storage at a controlled temperature. When we reach the end of October, we start to plow the fields ready for the November planting."

It is not the flowers, but the bulbs which are really the most important to the tulip-grower. A lot of people come to see the Roozen's tulips and to buy the bulbs – about a quarter of a million each year. They come from all over the world, and it is dealing with customers that takes up most of Leo's time, in all about sixty hours a week.

Left *A sea of color stretches as far as the eye can see.*
Below *The tulip bulbs are dried and stored ready for planting.*

A Dutch home

Leo invites us into the house for some refreshment, and we walk slowly back through the beautiful garden. The Roozen's modern, two-story house is larger than most Dutch homes. Holland is the most densely populated country in the world, and housing has always been a problem. In towns, people usually live in small modern apartments, or rooms in old terraced houses, and there is a small population of houseboat dwellers, too. Space is limited and a typical family home has one living room, three bedrooms, a kitchen and a small bathroom.

"Where are you?" calls Leo, as we go inside. Sylvia and the two children are in the dining room. Evelien and Bas are playing "doctors," and Evelien is lying on the polished wooden floor while Bas examines her.

"Please sit down," asks Sylvia. "Did you enjoy your tour?"

She offers us freshly-made coffee and sweet pastries. There are small toys on the floor and on the table are paper animal masks, which Sylvia has been helping the children to make.

"Doctor Bas" examines his patient, Evelien.

Bas and Evelien like it best when Sylvia joins in their games.

"I enjoy playing with the children, even though Bas is rather young at the moment. We do jigsaw puzzles, sing together and read fairy stories," she said.

Sylvia is 30 years old and a full-time housewife, looking after the house and bringing up the children.

"I like cooking, and being with the children while Leo works with the tulips. In that way, we share out the work.

"We get up about 7 o'clock each morning. Breakfast is different kinds of bread – brown, white and black rye bread – with butter, thin slices of cheese, peanut butter or jam. The children like *ontbijtkoek* (breakfast cake). We drink tea without milk and the children have milk or yogurt. Leo is at work by 8 or 8:30 am. And I take the children to school."

Bas and Evelien have run off to play on

Sylvia has a full-time job looking after the house and children.

a large rocking-horse in the spacious kitchen. They spend a lot of time playing in here while Sylvia is doing housework or cooking. They sit at the table and paint or draw, and sometimes make pastry. In the mornings, Evelien attends a kindergarten in nearby Vogelenzang, and Bas goes to a nursery school. It was Sylvia who took the initiative in starting the local nursery school.

"I simply phoned around to the young mothers in the village and asked them if they were interested in a nursery school, and many of them were. The nursery, which is three years old now, is open three times a week in a disused school. It costs only 2 guilders a session. So now we mothers can have some free time once in a while," she smiles.

Sylvia takes the children cycling

whenever she can, and if Leo has time he goes too. She and Leo greatly enjoy the countryside and nature, and want the children to grow up with the same enthusiasm.

"Loving nature is something that we are teaching our children. It is important to understand and respect it, and to live as part of it. When people are lumped together in big cities they lose contact with nature, and things start to go wrong. Crime increases, and people become discontented. I believe you can only keep your peace of mind if you are in contact with nature," explains Leo.

When Sylvia goes cycling, Bas and Evelien are not left behind.

A close family life is important to the Dutch. They are a very home-loving nation, preferring to spend their evenings in their own comfortable surroundings.

"I watch a lot of television," admits Leo, and a smiling Sylvia nods in agreement. "After a hard day's work, I like to relax completely! I also like to spend some time with the children, playing with them or reading to them before bed-time."

Sylvia prefers handicrafts. "I enjoy making lace, embroidery, crochet and knitting sweaters for the children."

She shows us some of the things she has made, including the curtains in the living room. Sylvia also owns a small movie camera, and she especially enjoys filming the children.

"We also play tennis," Sylvia smiled, "but not with each other. We did to begin with, but Leo kept on losing so he wouldn't play with me any more!"

Family ties are strong, and the Roozen's often get together with relatives for celebrations.

Left *Leo enjoys reading to the children.*
Right *Sylvia's favorite way of relaxing is to do handicrafts.*

"The most popular festival is St. Nicholas Eve," says Sylvia. "St. Nicholas is the patron saint of children – you will know him as Santa Claus. According to the legend he arrived from Spain by boat

St. Nicholas Eve is the most popular time of year with Dutch children.

24

and then rode high over the rooftops dropping presents down chimneys. The legend is still acted out today, and each year at the end of November, St. Nicholas arrives in Amsterdam with Black Peter, his servant. He is welcomed by the Burgomaster and then rides in procession through the streets crowded with children. We all exchange presents and eat and drink traditional fare. It's a real family occasion."

In his spare time, Leo is involved in education, too. He is on the committee of a private Catholic school, whose job is to choose the teachers, and to help decide the curriculum.

"We don't try to brainwash the children with religion, but we do believe that religious instruction is important, and hope the pupils will learn some moral values. Otherwise there is nothing special or different about the school," Leo told us.

Leo was called to take his place on the committee since, like 40 percent of the population, he is a Catholic. Holland has many different Catholic and Protestant groups who have their own schools, newspapers, social clubs, and so on. In the state schools, religion is not a compulsory subject.

Feeding the carp in the garden pool.

The family take their annual vacation in winter, since that is a quiet time in the tulip-growing industry. For the past few years they have been to Austria, because Leo is a passionate skier. This year, though, it is Sylvia's turn to decide. She would like them to go somewhere warmer!

Mealtime

Sylvia and Leo have invited us to join them for lunch, and while we have been talking a delicious aroma has been finding its way to us from the kitchen. In our honor, Sylvia has cooked a traditional Dutch dish, "Hunter's Roast." It is the family's favorite meal of beef cooked in herbs and red wine, topped with red cabbage, apples and potatoes.

Sylvia does her shopping in nearby Vogelenzang. There is a newly-opened supermarket there which she finds very convenient, but she also likes buying at the weekly village market.

We end our meal with sweet pancakes, a traditional treat, and Leo insists we try a glass of *genever* or Dutch gin. It's very strong!

Sylvia and Leo have known each other since they were in their teens. They have a very close relationship, and discuss everything, from problems with the children to major decisions about the business. Sylvia smiles as she remembers how they met.

"I went to a dance with a girlfriend. She told me about her boyfriend but I wasn't

"Hunter's Roast" is a traditional Dutch meal.

Leo and Sylvia first met when they were in their teens.

really interested and didn't take much notice. Later on I heard she had stopped seeing him.

"Then a friend asked me to her party and she said that this boy would be coming, and that I must meet him. I wasn't sure about that at all! I was very doubtful about meeting him, but I went to the party anyway. I met Leo and he was totally different from the person I had imagined. He was quite charming, and we fell in love! That's how we met!"

Sylvia and Leo got married in 1974. They had already known each other for a long time, and we asked them why they had waited before marrying.

Sylvia explained, "Leo fought against marriage for a long time. He was afraid of losing his freedom. But in the end it was Leo who wanted us to get married. He had been living abroad, in Stockholm. We wrote to each other every day! When he came home, he had made up his mind. He came straight to see me and said 'let's get married.'"

Leo smiled at this memory.

Sylvia spends a lot of time in the kitchen and she enjoys cooking.

It is time for us to leave. The whole family comes out on to the road to see us off. We thank them for their hospitality and shake hands with all of them. Just as we are about to go, Sylvia presents us with a large bunch of flowers, and Leo gives us some of his prize bulbs, as a souvenir of our day among the tulip fields.

A colorful array of beautiful flowers.

Facts about Holland

Size: The area of Holland is about 33,983 sq. km. (13,117 sq. mi).

Capital city: The capital of Holland is Amsterdam.

Population: There are about 14,091,014 people living in Holland.

Language: The language is Dutch.

Money: The Dutch buy their goods in kroners and guilders. There are 2.82 kroners to one guilder, and about 4.5 guilders to $0.33.

Religion: 40 percent of people are Roman Catholics, 30 percent are Protestants, and about 26 percent have no religion.

Climate: The climate in Holland is more or less the same throughout the country, although the northern parts are generally colder. In winter the temperature is around freezing point, and in the summer it is about 21°C (70°F).

Government: Holland is a constitutional monarchy. Its system of government is based on compromise, and is always formed by a coalition of up to five parties. Elections take place every four years. The Queen presides over the Council of State which advises on all legislation.

Education: Dutch children have to attend school between the ages of six and sixteen. However, there is good nursery school provision for 4–6 year olds. After school, children can go on to college or a university.

Agriculture: Holland produces milk, pork and bacon, chicken, beef, veal, eggs, vegetables, fruit, flowers, bulbs, sugar beets, potatoes, wheat, barley and oats.

Fishing: This has always been a strong Dutch industry and sole, herring, plaice, cod, turbot, shellfish, haddock, whiting and mackerel are caught.

Industry: Holland has the largest natural gas reserves in Western Europe. Its main industries are steel, shipbuilding, aircraft, cars, electronics, machinery, beer, tobacco, textiles, printing, diamonds and chemicals.

Glossary

Bloom Flower.

Bulb The enlarged underground stem of plants such as tulips daffodils and onions, which sends roots downward and leaves and flowers upward.

Burgomaster Mayor.

Carp A freshwater fish.

Cross-pollination Taking pollen from one flower and transferring it to another, usually by the action of wind or insects.

Dike A man-made bank, built as a barrier to stop flooding.

Kindergarten A class or small school for children usually between the ages of four and six.

Maritime Having to do with the sea.

Polder An area of land which has been reclaimed from the sea.

Robust Strong and healthy.

Variety A type of plant produced by artificial breeding.

Index

Acknowledgements

All the illustrations in this book were supplied by the authors, with the exception of the following: Netherlands National Tourist Office 7, 8, 9, 10. The maps on pages 7 and 11 were drawn by Bill Donohoe.

32